Always Here
Always Odd

Always Here Always Odd

poems

Garrett Buhl Robinson

Poet in the Park®
In Humanity I see Grace, Beauty and Dignity

"Hopeless Poem" appeared in October Hill Magazine, Fall 2018

cover photo and design by Garrett Buhl Robinson

Poet in the Park and the *Solemn Swan* colophon are trademarks registered with the United States Patent and Trademark Offices

Garrett Buhl Robinson © 2011, 2013, 2017, 2018 & 2019
All Rights Reserved

Poet in the Park
In Humanity I see Grace, Beauty and Dignity.

PoetinthePark.com

Contents

For Mom 1

Ways of Life

For John Ashbery 5
Coach 7
The Players Club 9
Perennial Spring 10
Touch Up 11
For Marshall Edwin Rosenstein 12
Sometimes All the Time 15
Landscape of Lyrics, Vineyards of Verse ... 16
Made of Music 17

Lit Figs

Lit Figs 21
Song and Circumstance 22
Proof of Life 23
Relatively Stable 24
For Ms. Bee 25
Artistry in Algebra 26
Routine 27
Maps Are Metaphors 28
This May 29
Jig 30
Always Here 31

Imaginary Material

All Essential	35
What It Is Is Its Worth	36
One is Always Odd	37
Hopeless Poem	38
Tiny	39
Vagabond Song	40
Voyager	42

Blue Print of the Sky

Drugs Are a Trap	45
Christmas Tree Song at New Year	46
The Presence of the Past	47
The View from my Cave	49

Emperor Norton in Love

Emperor Norton in Love	55

Afterword

Comments for My Poems?	73

For Mom

For Mom

Once, I saw my mom's hands still years ago,
perhaps the only time I've seen them rest
except at supper when our meals were blessed.
I've never seen the work of those hands slow,
spinning family flax into loving gold
and when she saw where my eyes had set
she confessed with modest self-consciousness,
"Isn't it awful the way the veins show?"

Mom, your hands are of a most gracious beauty.
Those veins are swollen from devoted work.
The wise guidance of those hands had raised me.
When I misbehaved they would make me smart.
The gentle care of those hands carried me
and will always hold me up to your heart.

Ways of Life

For John Ashbery

Reading John Ashbery is like chasing a fox
 through the forest.
I can see the nimble flash dashing and darting
 through the lush vegetation.
He slyly peaks around trees and then weaves
 through the swaying stands.
He'll crest a hill and then dives into a dale making
 waves with the landscape.
If I remain sharply focused, I can follow him
 through the turns
but I can never catch him,
till suddenly at the end of the last line
 — he vanishes.

Then I lift my gaze from the page and see
the world in a completely different way.

the lines rise
from the page
and slowly disappear

into the ever
clearer heights
of the sky

the sun withdraws
with her purple
and pink shawls

as one by one
the stars
populate the night

Coach

> — Totus mundus agit histrionem
> "All the World is a Playhouse."
> motto for The Globe Theatre

At times I think of players on the stage
and our endless fascination with games
in the intersecting fields of play where
William Shakespeare was able to portray
how the formal decorum of the Court
relates to situations every day.

I consider how games inspire young minds
and how Yogi Berra had coached my life
and although I was terrible at sports
— I never had the mind to play the games —
I was always astonished how the coaches
were masters of the proverbial phrase.

There is something to learn in every field
and what any involvement may reveal,
as we are products of interaction
and morality guides the way we play,
despite titles of losers and champions
the aim is really to stay in the game.

There are functions in the human circles
of industry, commerce, social service,
contemplation and application
but then I think of all the livelihoods sustained
and of every possible vocation
I most admire what keeps us entertained.

How we act produces society
for prosperity through posterity,
and what better impetus for creation
than the dynamics in which we engage
through every practical manifestation
found throughout the ingenious ways we play.

The Players Club
> — from a visit to Edwin Booth's Home

Mr. Booth, you had made the world your stage
but your home is a musical instrument.
It is the piece that continues to play
as the chambers resound with theatrics.
After the symposium the docent
led us through the bar and into the parlor
where Mark Twain had blown curly clouds of smoke
while holding crowds captive with savory stories.
Then as we ascended the stairs, each step
rose through the portraits of famous visitors,
yet, at the top, the wall next to your bed
is haunted with a picture of your brother.
Your room is unchanged since the night you died,
a script, a stage, a life preserved through time.

Perennial Spring

Ms. Millay, there is a wonder in poetry
that you have, a touch of life that patiently
sleeps in the pages awaiting to be awakened
with a reader's intrigue. The other night,
I found myself singing your verse again
and the lines touched upon my past
in ways I had forgotten, incidents
of little consequence, yet essential
for my own individual existence.
I was stumbling through the cellar of my mind
and found some seeds quietly hibernating.
I lifted them into the warm light
of your opening pages and they sprouted
with unfolding foliage then flowered
into fruition. The laurel twine of your lines
reaches a deep mystery in my life.

Touch Up

The speaker of this poem once saw someone
terribly tattered yet miraculously intact
stagger out of a dark place, perhaps a cave
or some other location of desperation.
For a moment the androgynous person paused,
bent over to pick up a piece of trash scuttling
along the ground and with the drops of tears,
made a watermark of verse. The speaker
remembered Ms. Dickinson composing
clavichord notes on everything she could find —
the leaves of plants she nurtured in her warm
garden until they bloomed into music.
In her hands, rubbish, refuse and otherwise
dispatched scraps turned into something beautiful.

For Marshall Edwin Rosenstein

From the bluster of burley work
    driving this big city
there was a soft and tender heart
    in quaint Greenwich Village.

There is the verdure of the trees
    overarching cobbled streets
with eccentric rows of homes
    rich with history.

Yet in the spirit of the past
    as we make our present way,
we are the most engaged
    with the history made today.

And of all the famous figures,
    the entire community
is what's required to weave
    this elaborate tapestry.

So when a single thread is lost
    that had weaved through all our lives,
the whole fabric is diminished
    and frays what once was tight.

There was a Marshall of this city
    who would calmly stroll these streets,
setting everyone at ease,
    a true officer of peace.

If you earnestly asked him
    he would tell about himself
yet by far his greatest interest
    was everybody else.

He would offer wise advice,
    his eyes shined beautifully,
and could settle all confusion
    with deep tranquility.

Everybody knew him,
    a local celebrity
famous for the quality
    of his humble empathy.

They may talk about the movers
    who push and pull and never tire,
but it's amazing how one kind person
    could touch so many lives.

He could light the sky with kindness,
    his smile was a song in itself,
he is carried on forever
    in his love for everyone else.

He was the one and only Marshall
    who calmly strolled these streets,
setting everyone at ease,
    a true officer of peace.

* * * * *

This poem was requested by a neighbor of Mr. Rosenstein.

Sometimes All the Time
    — for Jannika Viljanen

Even surrounded by a million people
    you feel the coldness of being alone
and all those times you can't keep still
    you think how far you've travelled from home.

You may not get the attention you deserve
    at the times you have something to say
and feel an insistent urge to be heard
    but everyone else just turns away.

There are times when we all doubt ourselves
    and feel vacant and drained from all we give,
but at times when everything seems to fail
    take just a moment to consider this —

Love can sometimes feel like sadness
    and I speak from experience,
yet every place you bless with your presence
    there is no end to the happiness.

Landscape of Lyrics, Vineyards of Verse

Horace sings at Sabine for all of time
as the wisdom of his rhythmic lines
perennially run just as his vines
to fill carafes with notes of his fine wine.

Over the dappled hills of the country side
a shiny fleet of clouds sail through the sky
while the tendrils nimbly continue to climb
as the bright ideas ripen in his mind.

Memories are weighed on the scales of music
as the recollections of experience
are measured with poetic metrics
and shared in the circling cups of expression.

He can still tickle the page with a pen
and make the blank space dance and laugh and sing.

Made of Music

Every day is amazing, and this one too
    since I had the rare opportunity
to meet the virtuoso Frederic Chiu
    at my bookstand in front of the library.

Immediately we were discussing
    the works of the French Impressionists
and with murmuring stirs of memories
    described the subtle palettes of music.

The conversation continued to unfold
    as we began to discuss Debussy
and the stories he told in tender tones
    yet as distinct as a typewriter's keys.

Or how he could sit at a piano
    and as if with a painter's hint present
the wondrous worlds he composed and evoked
    with the perfect touch of his fingertips.

And with melodies of art and beauty
    every single statement that we made
sounded to weave into a harmony
    arranged into a musical phrase.

Lit Figs

Lit Figs

A poem cannot build you an abode
but it may help to make you feel at home.

A poem cannot provide sustenance
but strengthens with inspired encouragement.

A poem cannot quench your thirst
but the fluency may refresh with verse.

A poem cannot turn on the lights
but a passage may open new insights.

A poem cannot heal the sick
but may comfort you through convalescence.

A pocm cannot teach you math
but may provide lines into the abstract.

This poem isn't worth any money.
It circulates and appreciates beauty.

Song and Circumstance

There is a bird in a field
and the bird is singing.

In Spring the field
is filled with flowers
and the bird is singing.

There is a war and the field
is scorched with clashing battle
and the bird is singing.

There is snow and the field
is covered with a frigid chill
and the bird is singing.

There is day, there is night,
there is the passage of time
and the bird is singing.

Proof of Life

Some have said the lines of a sonnet are
the bars of a jail, but this is simply
a matter of perspective. What I see
are the strings of an elegant harp.
I see rays of warmth leaping from the sun.
I see the steps of a flight of stairs that rise
into an opening door of love's delight.
I see the ripples of a river as it runs
from the headwaters of the Renaissance,
gathering in trickling rivulets
splashing laughter and meandering music.
I see the soft ribs of a celestial
being with a heart moving fluid life
and lungs swelling with the air that inspires.

Static Interaction

Although we cannot claim our first
conception every placement is a statement

in a seamless sequence of productions
of situation and circumstance.

We change as we are changed, impress as we
are impressed, study the world as we

are subject of it. In uncertain awareness,
we distinguish as the indistinguishable,

delineate as the indelineable –
a mass moving as it is moved through masses.

We keep our composure, for a time,
stabilized by our associations,

shaped and displayed in our involvements,
bonding in our energetic agreements,

but eventually thin in our existence
that stretches us out to the last line.

For Ms. Bee

I am terribly sorry little bee.
I certainly did not intend to tease
but the open flowers on the sleeves
of my books displayed so alluringly
are only the prints of photography.

While you buzz back and forth busily
I humbly offer an apology
because I know the nectar that you seek
is not the type of nectar on these leaves —
they are written to be read, not to eat.

With all your eyes I'm surprised you can't see
but you see a different world than me
and while I write sweet figures in poetry
you make your honey literally.

Artistry in Algebra
— for Chris Joyce
Fork Union Military Academy, September 1985

One of my fondest childhood memories:
on the towering top floor of Hatcher Hall,
Captain Joyce filled the room with classical
music while an oscillating fan wheezed
to stir the humid air into a breeze
over the rows of uniformed cadets
while we worked diligently at our desks.
Our brows speckled with sweat, we earnestly
struggled to solve the perplexing problem
for the worthy sake of an education —
exactly how to balance an equation
on the tip of a sharpened pencil.

* * * * *

I often tell people, "If you really want to be in the avant-garde,
don't be an Artist, be a Mathematician."

Routine

I have learned to love the blank page.
It is not a wall. Not a block of ice.
It is where I pour myself to make myself
exhaustless before the endless emptiness.
Slipping free from yesterday's dreams
I rise from my sleep and walk to the edge
of my desk to dive into a shallow sheet
of a leaf opening with my being
deepening with my singing, reminding me
that the benign is the twin of the sublime
while the scroll unrolls and dimensions
unfold with attention and invention.

Maps Are Metaphors

I have often thought of topography
to map the rough terrain of my life
where tight increments of lines steeply climb
and swiftly slide through creases of ravines
washing with the watersheds as they spread
in fanning planes that slip beneath the sloughs
of a glassy lake where the soft plop
from a raindrop sends ripples on the body
of water's settled, reflective repose
so the whole sky begins waving overhead.

Or perhaps these rings of lyrics outline
a mountain, tightening as they rise,
narrowing to one peak from every side
ascending to touch the attentive mind.

This May
> — For Lee Christine Brownlee

May your thoughts flourish with verse
and flutter with effortless ease
like the birds and butterflies
in the fragrant blooms of spring.

May your troubles calm
like a pond at dawn,
a mirror framed at the shore
where the willows' limber stems
bend to touch their reflection.

May the swans glide into the open
to rear in trumpeting majesty
then shake the mist from their wings
and running on their striding feet
leap into flight over uplifting trees.

Jig

My life remains a puzzle. My failure is the notion
that there is a solution. The missing pieces are
what I continue moving through, reaching
for an edge or a notch or someway
something will cinch. Nothing ever does.

I do recall — almost like the sweet memory
of my mother reading fairy tales before
my little ship set sail in a sea of dreams —
times when I had felt a sense of certainty.

Later, they always proved to be the soft
sinking of complaisant complacence.
Where I stop, I will be forever.
So I continue moving through the mystery
and sounding out my steps with poetry.

Always Here

There is a soaring image of a friend
and I would never dare to hold her back.
There are the most marvelous directions
open before her that in my own past
were blurred and obscured with my confusion
and I cannot retrace my staggering tracks,
the attempt would be another delusion.
Perhaps that is all I know for a fact.

Even if I don't have an audience
I will sing – the silence will be listening.
And if my parchment is oblivion
I will inscribe my lines on nothing.
Even if there is no gratification
I am assured I exist by persisting.

Imaginary Material

All Essential

There was a child who liked to sit at desks.
He would build models as the lines intersect
through the opening folds of schematic maps
instructing assemblies. He would spin tacks
and roll marbles, finding endless amusement
in the ways to build and sustain suspense.
Now, he weaves lines of music into text.
In the thin edge of paper he finds depth
and writes passages through blank surfaces.
Hearing an echo of Whitman he says,
"It is no greater or lesser than anything else."
and sets another book on the branch's shelf.
It is simply what he enjoys to do
and he has found others who like it too
and when people ask of the value of poetry
he says it broadens possibility.

What It Is Is Its Worth

I have been wandering off my whole life
composing my own literary line
with the plodding steps of my curious mind.
I sing exalted songs while I rise
then lament each darkening decline.
I have endured the switchbacks while I climbed
lifted my arms into the empty sky
before I tumbled down the other side.
Then I stand back up time after time.
Perhaps it is all there is worthwhile,
perhaps it's all I ever wanted in life,
but there is a brutal beauty I cannot deny
in the wandering wonder where I abide.
I will always explore till I expire.

One Is Always Odd

Many have said the world is relative
but every moment is exactly what it is
and there is a perfect continuity
transforming through all that exists.
Some places may seem exotic to some
but then are commonplace to another
but the opinions and tastes of one person
do not define the being of the other.
Most often I am an anomaly,
a melody wandering through the fog.
I am a song and I am a singing
in the music playing my whole life long.
Really, it is self-explanatory:
The individual is always odd.

Hopeless Poem

Sometimes I wonder if I am only
capable of making mistakes.
I always have the most uncanny
way to find precisely how anything breaks.
I've stepped off ledges while reaching for stars.
My bumbling always crumbles into jumbles.
I spend hours tuning stringless guitars
while boasting of times when I was humble.
I'll find something odd from the peas in a pod,
make a mess with nothing but emptiness.
Yet at least I know the roads I have trod
while I sing songs consoling the hopeless.
In the world's endless possibility,
failure is my failsafe consistency.

Tiny

Sometimes I feel my life is a tuneless string
of mistakes as I try to make sense of existence
from the scattered catastrophes of my past.
Really, I am more like a little grain of sand
tumbling in the surf at the edge of a vast
ocean beneath the endless sky at the shore
of an expansive continent. I know nothing
but the tumbling confusion of turning waves
at the intersection of infinite fields. So I think
of Blake and his grain of sand. And yes,
I believe he is right: a piece of infinity is
an infinite piece and we may all add to the endless.
So, I will be the grit of the grain, and in the oyster
of my tiny world I may gloss into a pearl.

Vagabond Song

There are endless paths for any travel
    and my vehicle is my rhyming feet.
There are destinations and arrivals
    but my journey will never be complete.

My wandering can easily be traced
    with villages and towns set on a string
but my destination is not a place,
    my goal is to continue to sing.

Once I heard the rumble of a carriage.
    The panels were polished, the accents gleamed
and the steeds pranced magnificently. Perhaps
    the coach was occupied by dignitaries

without a care but a singular intent
    to step directly from the velvet cushion
and onto some grand steps as they ascend
    into the majesty of a mansion.

I stepped aside to let the coach pass by
    as it struck a stone with a bumptious jolt
but built to ignore the rough road side
    the fortunate wheels continued to roll.

The dislodged stone haphazardly revealed
    a shiny key that had been buried beneath
and before me opened a door of my dreams
    not to arrive but continue travelling.

Voyager

With shelves of books and with the shelves themselves
I ribbed and sealed my hull and decked my craft.
Wonder is my prow, focus is my helm
and honest songs swell the sails of my masts
I made from my dock's straight and sturdy posts.
I know I won't need the dock anymore –
I can't commit myself into the open
if I try to keep one foot on the shore.
I am unmoored, I have found my release
into the ocean of eternity
with the schools of stars swimming through the deep
as I steer into the immensity.
I have become the ship, the sea, the wind
and I may never touch the land again.

Blue Print of the Sky

Drugs Are a Trap

In the oddest place
in the middle of a lake
floating
in the wide open
a fish found a worm
deliciously squirming
and could not resist
a savory nibble,
wanting nothing more
than to gobble it all
yet wondering
what it was tugging,
so sweet, so easy,
without seeing the barbed
hook embedded inside
and which most certainly
would snatch its life.

Christmas Tree Song at New Year

Yesterday I was everything.
They found me outside and circled around me with cheers.
They brushed the shivering snow from my verdant fir and stood me up in their home.
They adorned me with ornaments and strung lights from my outstretched limbs.
They set presents before me, gifts wrapped in beautiful paper, tied with velvet ribbons and knotted in elegant bows.
They crowned me with a sparkling star and gathered around me with mirth and merriment.
Then one morning they rushed up to me and tore the presents open and turned away with all their attention devoted to what had been concealed inside.
Then, with the gathered wrapping and packaging, they tossed me back outside.
Yesterday I was everything.
Now I am nothing.

The Presence of the Past

I do not even know when I left home.
In a way, I've always been on my own
for my whole life just like everyone else
in the solitary sense where we are all confined,
but sometimes I wonder if I ever left
or if I was ever there. Parts of me
will always remain intact and attached
to a place warmly residing in another time.
These are the comforting corridors of memory
where I may always rest and reflect
even while the bustling city teems above me
in the cannonball shots of the subway.

Recently, I visited again, slipping
into the warm folds of my parents' abode.
Most everything remains the same
and what is new seems to have always been
meant to be. Everything feels settled but I can
still sense the restless heave and heft
of my father. Every arrangement
is still warm with my mother's tranquil touch.
All they had carried now carries them.

In the morning, I sat on the porch
with my parents for their devotional.
The songs of birds filled the surrounding forest,
sweet little notes dripped from the tips
of rustling leaves. Squirrels hopped along the limbs,
their fluffy tails bobbing behind them.
My parents listened to the lessons explicating
the text and traced the twining lines of their life
along the verses of ancient scripture.

Afterwards, soaring on polished steel wings
back to my spot where I outline the loops
of my life day after day by running errands,
retrieving needs or just stepping outside for relief,
I received a message from my mother.
She said she keeps turning around to tell me
something, perhaps to offer the berry of an idea
or insight that had slowly ripened in her mind
and she plucked to give her child at just the right
time only to realize that I was already gone.

The View from my Cave

I don't understand how I can see
sound, how every object is humming
with meaning as if urging to open
into music. Sometimes the air is filled
with gossamers, little quivering strings
floating in ever changing arrangements.
I touch them with the tip of my pen,
tie them to the frame of a page
then tune them into a harp
some reader may play.

Emperor Norton in Love

Self-appointed as the Emperor of the United States and Protector of Mexico, Joshua Abraham Norton is a 19th Century folk hero who lived most of his life in San Francisco. A merchant who lost his fortune in a single shipment, he spent years on the streets entertaining people with his charisma and charm, living almost exclusively upon the goodwill of others.

Of the numerous stories told of his life, this poem describes an instance when he heroically deterred an angry mob from rampaging through the city. As the mob marched through the street, he stood directly in their path and brought them to a halt by reciting the Lord's Prayer. He continued to repeat the prayer until the crowd dispersed and peacefully returned to their homes.

This ballad also comically explores the issue of how unconventional and outright odd lifestyles may contribute to the benefit of society as a whole.

When he died in 1880, his funeral procession consisted of thousands of people. To this day, stories of Emperor Norton still delight the lives of residents and visitors of San Francisco.

Emperor Norton in Love

On yet another sunny day
    on Broadway at North Beach
the Royal Emp'ror Norton
    can once again be seen.

And on this day as every day
    a crowd has gathered round
as if they have been magnetized
    by melodies of sound.

But more than just his tone of voice
    there is a charming sight,
the same as the enchanting way
    that life is drawn to light.

The people's cheeks will blush rose red,
    their faces shine with smiles
and sometimes you can almost see
    the sun rise in their eyes.

But then there is a scuffling huff
    as shoves disturb the crowd
while someone pushes his way through
    with scowls of his dour frown.

The man proclaims an urgent task
    to which he must attend
but all he ever seems to do
    is insult and offend.

Each person has direction,
    a voice for their own say,
but all this guy has ever said
    is: "You're all in my way!"

It's like he has a special call
    for others to feel worse
and this begrudging task in life
    is his resolved purpose.

But the reigning Emp'ror Norton
    cannot be pushed aside,
the solid place of his stature
    is firm where he resides.

And complicating even more
    this man's repellency,
is Norton tends to embrace all
    who are within his reach.

So even in his grumbles,
    the man may squirm and tug
but finds himself warmly locked up
    in Norton's royal hug.

Released from Norton's warm embrace
    he's lighter on his feet
and all the bitter spite of life
    has suddenly turned sweet.

He staggers back in his surprise
    tongue tied for what to say
at how that gesture of acceptance
    brightened his glum day.

And suddenly astonishment
    about the quickened change
has turned his life so that he sees
    the world in a new way.

Then fumbling for some awkward words
    to fit into a phrase
he asks how Emp'ror Norton
    had cured him of his rage.

His day was ruined from the start
    before he left his bed.
As soon as he opened his eyes
    he felt a dismal dread.

We all have obligations
    along obstructed paths
and all his snarling obstacles
    would never let him pass.

The sunny fields beyond the hills
    that he had sought to find
were always blighted with the night
    the time that he arrived.

He found the gentle Emperor
    was standing in his way
but somehow Norton had transformed
    cold night into warm day.

Is this event a miracle?
    There's some who'd make that claim.
Yet Emperor Norton calmly says
    it's easy to explain:

"Don't feel you must deal like with like,
    a measure for a measure,
the way to truly conquer hate
    is with a friendly gesture."

But then the crowd was quite perplexed
    at Norton's noble stand
and how he mustered up the spunk
    to face the troubled land.

Incredulous a man protests
    if love can conquer hate
and doubtful that it can be done
    he has these words to say.

"Our lives are very complicated
    and answers are not clear,
it is a foolish strategy
    to laugh off hate and fear.

"There are the raging fires of war,
    aggressive, angry powers,
one cannot hope to make the peace
    by waving round a flower.

"And even if a person could,
    the act would still disrupt,
that poor, defenseless, helpless plant
    still had its flower plucked.

"How did the flower make offense?
    Whatever is the reason?
To make the knives turned on the plant
    and hack it into pieces?

"Our history has always shown
    what's innocent and nice
is always first to be led to
    the bloody sacrifice."

Then Emp'ror Norton calms the crowd
    with nothing but a sigh,
then with the twinkle in his eye
    presents his tickled smile.

The crowd moves closer so to hear
    how Norton will reply
and listens tight with all their might
    expecting something wry.

Then after a suspenseful pause
    the picture is reframed
as Norton soothes the patient crowd
    and tranquilly explains:

"The quibbling can go on forever
    to parse infinity,
but yet the truth often eludes
    our rationality.

"I'm one who does admire the plants,
    the flowers and the fruits,
the branching tips of tender stems,
    the deepening of roots.

"The flowers bloom so to allure
    with fragrant nectars sweet,
and I believe they're best admired
    with plants still in one piece.

"We cannot claim we love something
    then clip it for our use.
The life must stay complete and whole
    to thrive and to produce.

"Of course this is beside the point,
    please don't let me digress
but often the tangential thoughts
    enlighten and impress.

"Besides this little floral flourish,
    the question that you asked
is can a peaceful disposition
    divert a fierce attack?

"And keep in mind that this is not
    a futile abstract tactic.
This theory has been smartly proved.
    I've put it into practice.

"One night there was an angry mob
    that marched throughout the city,
they were determined to destroy
    without a drop of pity.

"They were all irked and riled about
    our life's humiliations
and they all sought to dissipate
    their furious frustrations.

"Too often when we're aggravated
    our anger turns to shame
because we often turn our rage
    on those who aren't to blame.

"This mob with torches in their hands
    were crazed to burn things down
and stormed the city streets that night
    inciting the whole town.

"I faced the mob right in the street,
    before the flickering flames,
I knew none of them were themselves
    but crazy with their rage.

"Then where I stood they stopped their march
    with stunned, bewildered stares
and then I started to recite
    the lines of the Lord's Prayer.

"I knew I was against the worst,
    it had to get much better
and then I reached the final line
    concluding with forever.

"When I recited the whole prayer
    up to the very end,
I then returned to the first line
    to say it once again.

"Again, again I said the prayer
    to hot and angry faces,
and slowly watched the fearsome heat
    cool into sweetened graces.

"Then slowly all the raucous noise
    was peaceful in no time,
so calm we thought that we could hear
    stars twinkling in the sky.

"The flames still burned, but differently,
    a change in wind was blown,
the flames would not burn down the town,
    their light now led them home."

But then another rousing voice
    has yet another question
as if the crowd ceaselessly craves
    Norton's explanations.

"Your story's sweet and wonderful
    except for just one word —
How could the Royal Emperor
    be subject to a Lord?"

The Emperor took pause again
    and arches up his brow.
Not curious at what they asked
    but puzzled by their doubt.

Then with a single sip of wine
    to tune his vocal chords
he opens up the sluice again
    for his profuse discourse —

"We all have guides to all our lives
    of this you can believe
and I am subject to these rules
    since I had been conceived.

"Those rules align our different lives
    so we may interact,
then we can compensate each other
    for what we each may lack.

"The shops of bakers have the bread,
    the butchers have the meat.
The vaulted banks secure the cash
    and trolleys rest our feet.

"But when regarding our positions
    refrain from hasty judgement,
those who are held to be up high
    have others up above them.

"And as the ruling Emperor,
    there's something you must see,
I'm really not up on the top
    but under everything.

"And all my grandeur and my grace
    and willingness to please
is for my station's dedication
    to the noblesse oblige.

"I march around like a parade
    in step with my own time
but underneath my plum panache
    you'll find my humble mind.

"I'm working all the day and night
    performing dutifully,
there is no way I will neglect
    responsibilities.

"And if I strayed for just a wink
    so my attention lapsed,
there is a terrible concern
    the world might then collapse."

Then with this claim there is a stir,
    that grumbles with discord,
and one voice speaks above the rest
    to ask for a report.

"Please tell us Emp'ror Norton,
    we'd love to hear you say
exactly what this service is
    that saves us every day.

"Each day we see you in the streets,
    each night you're in the bar,
what is this duty you perform
    that lights our guiding star?"

Perhaps the question was too easy
    and served up on a platter
but Norton gobbled it right up
    with dollops of his laughter.

"Have not you seen day after day
    and spanning the whole year
how tirelessly I work away
    to keep all in good cheer?

"I know some try to criticize
    and call it frivolous,
this isn't idle jollity
    or wasteful silliness.

"Every city has a hospital,
    and this I know is true
that getting people to feel better
    is what they're made to do.

"Our health is how we feel,
    I'm not just having fun,
the service I provide is real
    and helps out everyone.

"My prescription is for merriment,
    is that not understood?
I'm helping us to not feel bad
    by making us feel good.

"And if you ask who is my Lord
    it's not one up above,
it is something that's in us all —
    our Everlasting Love.

"Love is the most tenacious force
    for all society
and just as universal
    as Newton's gravity.

"Some people say it's of the mind,
    and others of the heart,
without it though there is no doubt
    we'd quickly fall apart.

"It can compel us while it binds us
    and guides us through our lives.
It is a vital quality
    to help us to survive.

"Sometimes it comes quite easily,
  you hardly have to try,
like when you brighten someone's day
  with a friendly smile."

Then Emp'ror Norton turns around
  and whiskers on his way,
fulfilling all his errant quests
  with his good deed today.

Some say he's Don Quixote,
  the Falstaff for his day,
but Royal Emp'ror Norton
  is unique in every way.

Afterword

Comments for My Poems?

With the submission of my poems
I found your request for comments
to be a source of bafflement.
How am I to corroborate
on what my poems have to say?
Their content is self-evident
and though I may have an intent
to what the phrases represent
the readers must have their own sense
as to what they mean to them.
So in response to the request you sent
I will be absolutely consistent
in fulfilling the redundant
and say: this is where this statement ends.

Also by Garrett Buhl Robinson

<u>Poetry</u>
Pilgrims
Whispering Emily
Little Pieces of Poetry
The Ballad of Emperor Norton
City of Poems
A Man Who Lives in a Dream
The Nobody
Beauty beyond Reason
Martha, a poem

<u>Fiction</u>
Zoë
Nunatak

<u>Musical</u>
Letters to Zoey

PoetinthePark.com

www.ingramcontent.com/pod-product-compliance
Lightning Source LLC
Chambersburg PA
CBHW060341080526
44584CB00013B/867